Contents

Getting started

- 3. How to use my journal ☐
- 5. Our Essential Agreements ☐
- 6. My learner profile ☐
- 8. Reflecting on the learner profile ☐

Self-management skills

- 10. Practising mindfulness ☐
- 11. Understanding my brain ☐
- 12. Regulating my emotions ☐
- 13. Taking action ☐
- 14. Managing emotions ☐
- 16. Managing anger and resolving conflict ☐
- 17. Taking action ☐
- 18. Identifying perseverance ☐
- 20. Practising perseverance ☐
- 22. Taking action ☐

Social skills

- 23. Social-emotional intelligence ☐
- 24. Being aware of myself and others ☐
- 25. Understanding responsibility ☐
- 26. Accepting responsibility ☐
- 27. Advocating for myself and others ☐
- 28. Taking action ☐
- 29. Interpersonal relationships ☐
- 30. Understanding collaboration and co-operation ☐
- 31. Reflecting on my role in a learning community ☐
- 32. Encouraging group collaboration ☐
- 33. Managing collaboration ☐

Thinking skills

- 34. Being reflective ☐
- 36. Considering and recording my progress ☐
- 38. Considering lessons and skills ☐
- 39. Critical and creative thinking ☐
- 40. Analysing and connecting information ☐
- 41. Proposing and evaluating solutions ☐
- 42. Taking action ☐
- 43. Transfer ☐
- 44. Taking action ☐

Research skills

45. Information literacy .... ☐
46. Understanding questions .... ☐
47. Formulating relevant questions...... ☐
48. Evaluating and choosing
    information and tools .... ☐
49. Media literacy .... ☐
50. Using media to gather
    information .... ☐
51. Choosing tools and platforms .... ☐
52. Taking action................................ ☐
53. Citing references .... ☐
54. Ethical use of media literacy.......... ☐
56. Using media ethically.................... ☐
57. Taking action................................ ☐

Communication skills

58. Exchanging information .... ☐
59. Following instructions.................... ☐
60. Understanding feedback .... ☐
61. Giving and receiving constructive
    criticism....................................... ☐

62. ICT: forms of communication......... ☐
63. Communicating using ICT .... ☐
64. Literacy: the power of written
    language....................................... ☐
65. Using literacy to communicate....... ☐
66. Communicating using technology... ☐
67. Taking action................................ ☐
68. Taking action using the SDGs.......... ☐
72. Expressing ideas and opinions:
    the SDGs .... ☐

Final reflections

75. Reviewing my exhibition .... ☐
77. Reflecting on my year.................... ☐
79. What's next?................................. ☐
80. Calming the mind with our
    breath .... ☐

How to use my journal

Welcome

This is your journal. Please use it to draw or write your ideas and thoughts.

There are no right or wrong answers – be free to explore.

The activities can help you to:

 Develop your **reflective** thinking skills.

Reflection can be …

Being aware of the present.
Describing your feelings.

Wondering.
Giving your perspective. Making connections.

Thinking back on your day.
Thinking forward about how to improve.

Planning goals for yourself and next steps.
Planning how to apply your skills to take action.

> Reflection involves all the **essential elements** (perhaps not all at the same time!)
> - Knowledge
> - Concepts
> - Skills
> - Learner profile
> - Action

 Reflect on and develop your learner profile attributes.

3

How to use my journal

 Assess your approaches to learning skills.

 Self-management skills – Be organized and manage your different states of mind.

 Social skills – Understand other people and how to work together.

 Thinking skills – Be critical and creative, think about how we think, and understand how we can use what we have learned to help us with new learning.

 Research skills – Use different methods to find information and understand how to use media safely and responsibly.

 Communication skills – Exchange information using different forms of literacy and Information and Communication Technology (ICT).

 Set **SMART** goals.

> **S**pecific: Be clear about what you want to do. Answer the questions: Who? What? Where? Why? Which?
>
> **M**easurable: Set a goal you can measure (How much? How many?).
>
> **A**ttainable: Aim to do something that's not too hard (or too easy).
>
> **R**elevant: Keep your goal related to what you want in the future.
>
> **T**ime: Decide when you will achieve your goal (and try to stick to it).

 Consider your progress.

 Take action!

Our Essential Agreements

Reflect on these questions:

- What do you need to learn successfully?
- What would your ideal classroom look like?
- What behaviour do you want to see in class?
- What routines help your learning?

Discuss with a partner and record your ideas.

 How do your ideas compare with your classmates' ideas?

My learner profile

Reflect on your learner profile. Which attributes are your strengths? Why?

1

2

3

Which attributes would you like to develop this year?

How might you start to do this?

Talk to a partner about your plan for the year.

Do they have any other ideas for how you could develop these attributes?

Reflecting on the learner profile

1. When Melati and Isabel were 10 and 12 years old, they had a lesson about positive world leaders. This inspired them to take action. They decided to help reduce plastic pollution in Bali.

2. In their research, they learned that less than 5% of plastic bags in Bali were being recycled.

3. In 2013, they set up their campaign 'Bye Bye Plastic Bags'. They organized clean-ups, presentations and they gave out alternatives to plastic bags.

4. In 2015, they began a **petition** asking the government to help. This was signed by 100,000 people.

2000	2002	2013	2015
Melati is born	Isabel is born	They set up 'Bye Bye Plastic Bags'	They begin a petition

 Which learner profile attributes have Melati and Isabel shown? Have they shown different attributes at different times of their lives? Write your thoughts under the timeline.

8

5 Following their work, **Bali's governor** finally agreed to meet them and promised to make Bali plastic bag-free.

6 In 2018, they led Bali's biggest beach clean-up. 20,000 people collected 65 pounds of waste.

7 Melati and Isabel helped build support by speaking at conferences, including the United Nations World Oceans Day in New York City. Their work, combined with the work of people who felt the same way, finally resulted in the ban of single-use plastic bags in Bali in 2019.

8 'Bye Bye Plastic Bags' now has over 50 teams around the world. In 2020, Melati created a company called YOUTHTOPIA to train and encourage young people to make changes.

2018	2019	2020	Today
They lead a beach clean-up	Single-use plastic bags are banned	Melati sets up YOUTHTOPIA	

Bali's governor person in charge of the government of Bali
petition something that people add their names to in order to show their support

Practising mindfulness

You are going to do a mindfulness practice.

Listen to your teacher read 'Calming the mind with our breath'.

How did it feel? What did you notice? Record your reflections.

Understanding my brain

Knowing how your amazing brain works will help you practise mindfulness and make calm decisions when you're feeling strong emotions.

The prefrontal cortex is our thinking brain. It makes good choices and helps us learn.

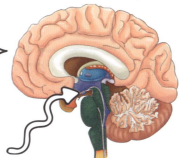

The amygdala keeps us safe by reacting to things it thinks are dangerous. We might react with strong emotions and feel sorry about it later.

Think about some times when we might react with the amygdala and not be able to think clearly. Record your ideas.

Regulating my emotions

Understanding our emotions can help us to regulate them, meaning we make changes to help control them.

Reflect on a time when you reacted with your amygdala (strong emotions) and a time when you responded with your prefrontal cortex (clear and mindful).

I reacted with my amygdala when …

I responded mindfully with my prefrontal cortex when …

Taking action

Think about what you know about mindfulness and managing emotions.
- ☐ Where could you go to calm down and regulate your emotions?
- ☐ What might you do to help yourself calm down?

 How could a regular mindfulness practice help you?

Managing emotions

Strong emotions can be caused by different events or thoughts. Things that cause negative emotions are sometimes called triggers. Things that cause positive emotions can be called glimmers.

Triggers

- Quick reactions from our amygdala
- Cause us to feel unsafe
- Cause big emotions like fear, anger or worry
- Signal stress in our body

List some of your triggers. What causes you to feel upset, angry, sad or scared?

How might knowing your triggers and glimmers help you at school?

14

```
                    Glimmers
                   / | | \
Tell us we're safe  | |  Help move us out of
                    | |  negative emotions
                    ↓ ↓
     Help us feel aware    Can be small things that
     of where we are       bring us happiness
```

List some of your glimmers. What causes you to feel safe, calm and peaceful?

How could knowing your triggers and glimmers help you be a better friend?

Managing anger and resolving conflict

Managing emotions includes recognizing when there is conflict, such as an argument, then trying to resolve the argument.

Look at this picture.
Think about triggers and glimmers.

What would you do to resolve the argument?

 Have you ever been in a situation like this?
What did you do? What could you do next time?

Taking action

What did I learn about self-management?

How can I use what I've learned?

What questions do I have?

What action can I take?

Identifying perseverance

Reflect on this story.

Circle wants to build a tower with his shape friends, but none of his ideas work.

Circle is almost ready to give up …

What might Circle do next?

What learner profile attributes connect with perseverance?

What approaches to learning connect with perseverance?

With a partner, research perseverance and resilience.
How are they similar? How are they different?

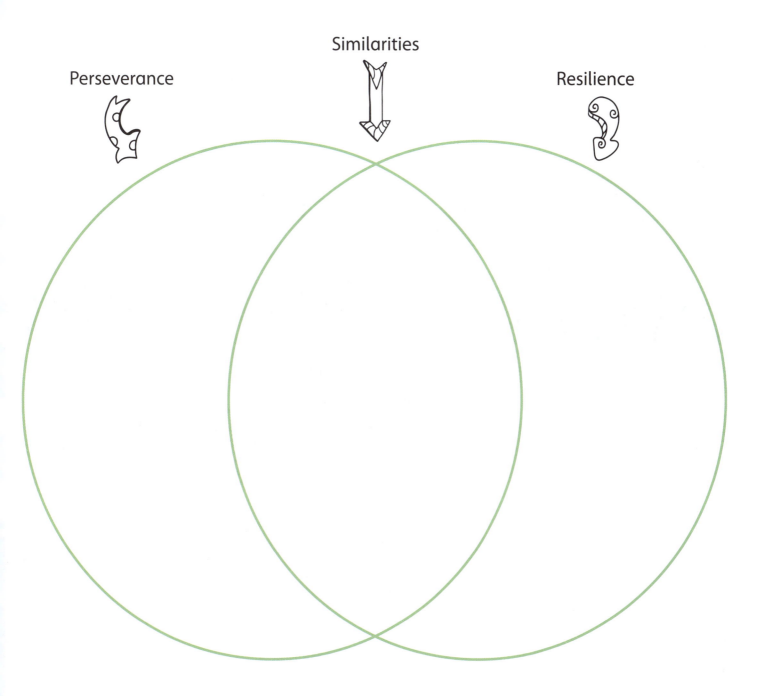

 When have you practised perseverance?
When have you shown resilience?

Practising perseverance

'The Learning Pit' shows the journey of learning something new.

 Discuss the picture with a partner. Share times when you felt like you were in 'the Learning Pit'.

How might knowing about 'the Learning Pit' help?

Think about your journey through the exhibition or an inquiry.
- ☐ Draw yourself at different points of your learning journey.
- ☐ Add thought bubbles to show how you felt.

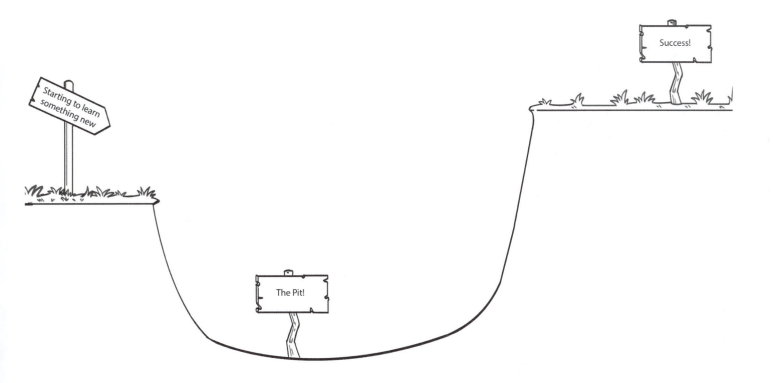

 Who helped you in the pit?

21

Taking action

Think about something difficult that you are working on.
Where are you in 'the Learning Pit'?

This is not as easy as I thought.

I'm confused.

Great! I understand it now!

How can I show perseverance in my learning?

What can I do when it gets difficult?

Social-emotional intelligence

When we are aware of ourselves and think about how we might affect other people, we show social-emotional intelligence.

What kind of learner are you?

Complete the bar chart to show how much you like each style.

Visual: I prefer to see pictures and to show my learning.
Solitary: I prefer to work alone.
Social: I prefer to work with others.

Physical: I prefer to use my body.
Logical: I prefer to work in clear steps.
Verbal: I prefer to learn by speaking, listening and reading.

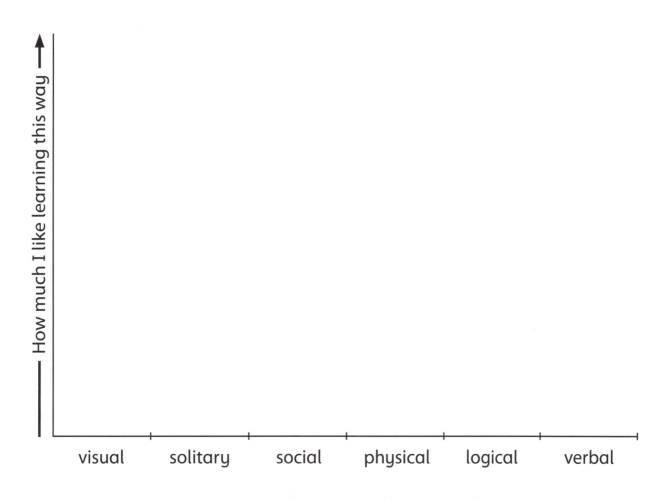

 Compare your chart with a partner's chart. What do you notice?

Being aware of myself and others

Taking action often involves collaboration, which means working together as a team.

To work well together, it is important that we understand the special qualities that each individual brings.

When we understand others, it is easier to manage our relationship with them and collaborate effectively.

- ☐ Look at this chart, which shows the learner profile attributes of another student.
- ☐ Reflect on their unique attributes. How easily might you work with this person? What might be difficult for you?

■ Risk-taker
■ Knowledgeable
■ Principled
■ Inquirer
■ Open-minded
■ Communicator

 What challenges have you faced when working with a partner or in a team? How has collaboration helped your learning? Discuss your thoughts with a partner.

24

Understanding responsibility

Write your own definition of responsibility.

> "Responsibility is accepting that you are the cause and the solution of the matter."
>
> *Anonymous*

Share your definition with a partner. How is theirs similar? How is it different?

Accepting responsibility

Reflect on the quote and record your thoughts.

> "The moment you accept responsibility for *everything* in your life is the moment you gain the power to change *anything* in your life."
>
> Hal Elrod

How do you show responsibility around others?

What might make you more responsible?

Advocating for myself and others

Advocating is supporting and speaking up for someone or something you believe in.

Choose a problem or topic you feel strongly about and use the 'action cycle' to plan how to advocate for yourself or others.

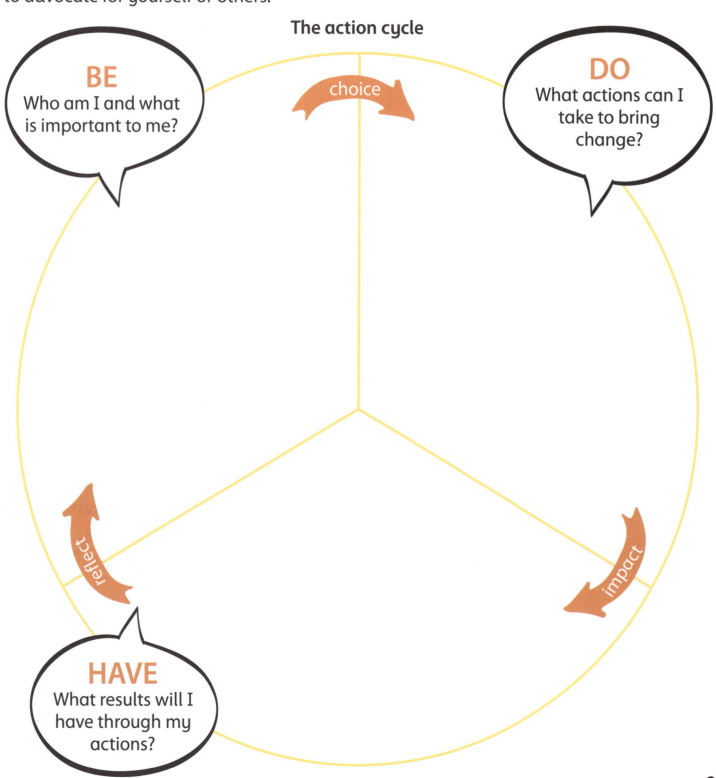

The action cycle

BE — Who am I and what is important to me?

DO — What actions can I take to bring change?

HAVE — What results will I have through my actions?

choice · impact · reflect

Taking action

Reflect on the skills you've been building.

- Resolving conflict
- Understanding myself and others
- Accepting responsibility
- Advocating for myself and others

How could I use these skills to help myself?

How could I use these skills to help others?

Interpersonal relationships

Who are you connected with? Record your thoughts in the chart.

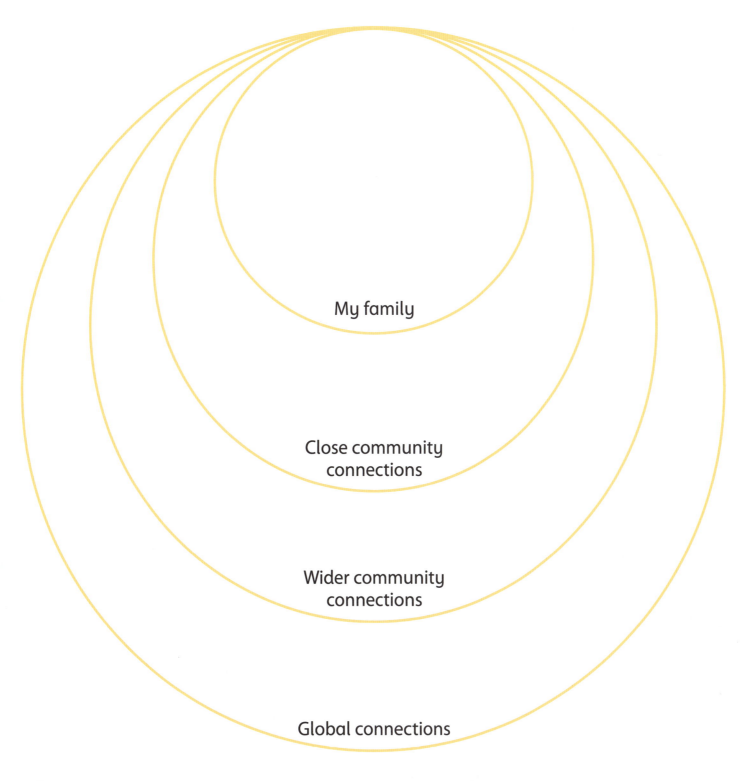

- My family
- Close community connections
- Wider community connections
- Global connections

 How do relationships help you to connect to people in your community? How do they help you connect to the wider community and to the world?

29

Understanding collaboration and co-operation

Co-operation means being helpful when we're working together.

Rate your level of co-operation this week on the line below.
Draw an arrow to show how co-operative you were.

⟵─────────────────────────⟶

I need to be more
co-operative

I was very
co-operative

Why did you rate yourself like this?

 Talk to a partner about what collaboration looks like to you.

Reflecting on my role in a learning community

1. Think about your learner profile attributes. Which ones describe you best?
2. Write them in the 'Key' below.
3. Make a pie chart of your learner profile attributes using different colours. The largest part shows your strongest attribute.
4. Colour the squares in the key to match your pie chart.

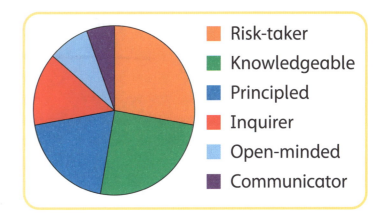

- Risk-taker
- Knowledgeable
- Principled
- Inquirer
- Open-minded
- Communicator

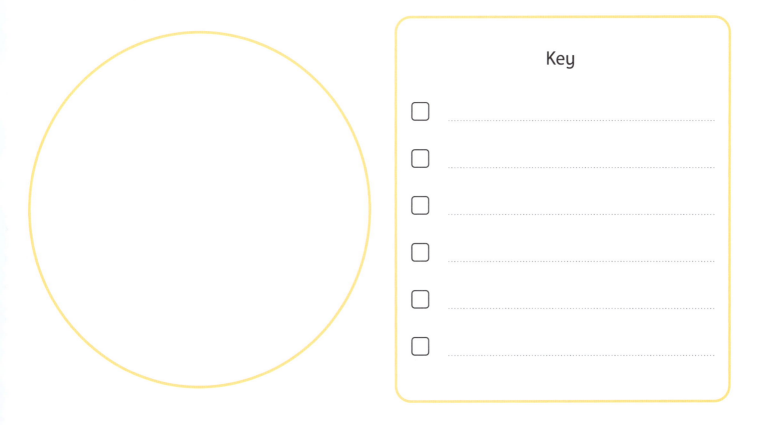

Key

Share your results with your group. Compare, contrast and discuss. Which roles in a group would suit each of you best?

Encouraging group collaboration

Reflect on this quote and record your thoughts.

> "Coming together is a beginning.
> Keeping together is progress.
> Working together is success."
> *Henry Ford*

What problems can there be with group work?

What solutions can you suggest?

Problems	Solutions

Managing collaboration

> Effective collaboration requires co-operation and delegation. This means giving out tasks to everyone.

- Think: What is the task or project?
- Reflect: What are everyone's strengths?
- Plan: What roles are needed for the task?
- Discuss: How do we delegate tasks?

Our task/project: ....

....

Fill in the jigsaw pieces with members of your group.
What role might they be best at?

Team member:

Role:

Team member:

Role:

Team member:

Role:

Team member:

Role:

Being reflective

Imagine you could do, have or be anything. What action would you take to help the world?

What you have just done is **reflective** thinking.

- Analyse: You reflected on your background knowledge, connecting with your future thinking.
- Draw conclusions: Next, you thought about what or where you could improve or change.
- Make an action plan and set goals: Finally, you considered positive, future-centred goals.

Reflect on this quote by John Dewey. Record your thoughts.

> "We do not learn from experience ... We learn from reflecting on experience."
> *John Dewey*

What attributes are involved in being **reflective**?

Considering and recording my progress

- ☐ Reflect before, during and after your learning journey this year.
- ☐ Use this list to judge your skills.
- ☐ Colour the boxes as you feel your skills are developing.

> 🟩 I am confident.
> 🟧 I am developing this skill.
> 🟥 I need more help with this skill.

Social skills	Before	During	After
I think before I act.			
I work co-operatively with others.			
I listen to others' opinions.			
I am responsible for my actions.			
I can identify my strengths and the things I find difficult.			

Research skills	Before	During	After
I analyse and draw conclusions from my data.			
I can find information related to my inquiry.			
I can organize data into categories such as tables, descriptions and diagrams.			
I can create key questions and supporting questions to make my research deeper and more useful.			

Thinking skills	Before	During	After
I am creative with my ideas.			
I think critically and solve problems.			
I can think about how I think (my metacognition).			
I reflect on my learning and plan steps for future success.			
I transfer my knowledge and understanding across my learning.			

Communication skills	Before	During	After
I listen to others.			
I take turns in discussions.			
I can express my ideas in different ways.			
I am confident and clear when I speak in front of an audience.			
I can communicate my learning using different forms of media.			

Self-management skills	Before	During	After
I can act responsibly.			
I can keep my materials organized.			
I can be patient and wait my turn.			
I get things done on time.			
I practise strategies to support mindfulness.			

Considering lessons and skills

What important lessons have you learned from your experiences so far this year?

Lesson learned	Who or what taught you this lesson?

- ☐ Consider your attitude to learning skills.
- ☐ Reflect on how you've grown this year.
- ☐ Colour the bar chart to show your progress.

Growth ↑

What advice would you give yourself for the future?

38

Critical and creative thinking

What is critical thinking? What is creative thinking? How do they compare?

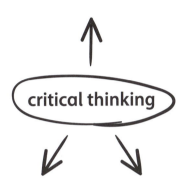

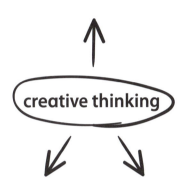

Metacognition is thinking about how you think.

Solve this problem:

> Amrit is looking at a photo of someone. He says: "I don't have any brothers or sisters, but this man's father is my father's son."
>
> Whose photo was Amrit looking at?
>
> Answer:

Identify your metacognition. What were you thinking?

Analysing and connecting information

Choose one of the pictures that interests you.

What do you already know?

What do you wonder?

How might the picture you chose connect with your current unit of inquiry?

Proposing and evaluating solutions

Thinking creatively helps us propose (come up with) solutions to problems. Next, we need to evaluate them (decide if they are good and might work).

- ☐ Analyse these action cycles.
- ☐ Reflect on the parts that you feel work best.
- ☐ Record your thoughts below.

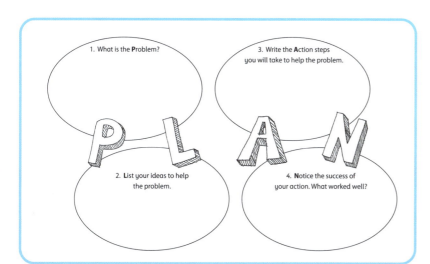

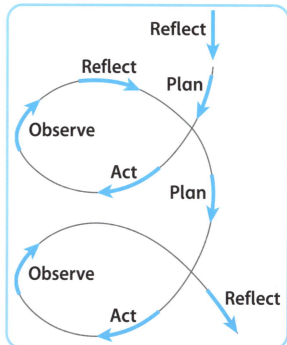

41

Taking action

Create your own diagram of an action cycle to teach others what it means to take action.

Transfer

When you start something new, think about how you learned something before. Remember knowledge you collected, strategies you used and skills you learned. Could these help with your new learning?

My last inquiry   **My new inquiry**

Our central idea: ....

....

....

Reflect on the knowledge, strategies and skills that you have used to support your learning throughout your inquiry.

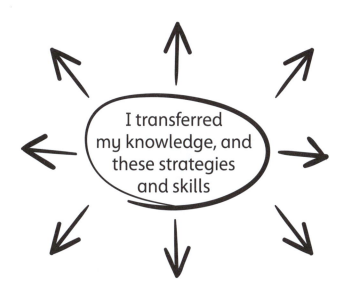

43

Taking action

How could your thinking skills be used in the real world?

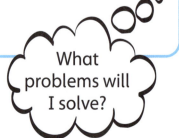

Information literacy

Information literacy means being able to find information and decide if it is useful.

How do you feel about your research skills?

What do you NEED to know?

What WORRIES you about this?

What EXCITES you about this?

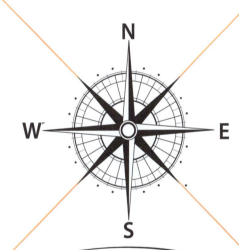

What might your next STEPS be? What SUGGESTIONS could you make?

Understanding questions

What makes a good question?
- ☐ Discuss your thoughts with a group. Write different people's ideas below.
- ☐ Use the ideas to help formulate great questions.

Formulating relevant questions

Formulating questions is the first step to planning our research. We want a balanced set of questions to produce a balanced inquiry.

Reflect on your questions and write them in the correct boxes.

Question type	Explanation	Example	My examples
Factual	Can be answered with a fact from somewhere like a book or the internet.	Who does Khalid live with?	
Predictive	Uses information from a text, or your own knowledge, to predict the answer.	Will Khalid find the strange door again?	
Analytical	Breaks down the information and looks for connections to the world, other texts or different data.	At what age is it safe for children to go out on their own?	
Synthesis	Uses what you've learned to create new ideas.	How else could the story have ended?	

47

Evaluating and choosing information and tools

Plan your research journey for your inquiry.

Type of research	How useful is this for my inquiry?	How could I use it?
Media Searching in books or websites		
Interview Reading interviews with experts or doing my own		
Survey Asking questions to find out what people think or do		
Observation Watching or noticing what happens in experiments, social situations, nature, art		

How do you feel about your media literacy skills?

Beginning	Developing	Independent
I can:	I can:	I can:

Media literacy

Research is like being a detective. There are many forms of media that we can use. Our job is to choose the best. This is media literacy.

Look around your classroom. Record sources of information that could help you.

 What new forms of media would you like to try?

Using media to gather information

Reflect on your media literacy.
- ☐ Think about the sources of information you have used in your research.
- ☐ Decide if the sources are primary or secondary and write them in the correct category.
- ☐ Reflect on your experience using each category.

	My examples	My reflection
Primary source The author of the source was there when the event happened.		
Secondary source The author of the source was NOT there when the event happened.		

Choosing tools and platforms

- ☐ Think about the resources, technology and skills you could use to present your research.
- ☐ How would you use them?
- ☐ Record your ideas below.

Resources or technology:

You could use programmes to make videos or slideshows. What else?

Other skills:

You might have useful skills in drama, science, problem solving, interviewing, creative design or music.

51

Taking action

What big problem would you like to solve?

....

....

....

....

You could think about the United Nations Sustainable Development Goals (SDGs). (pages 68–74)

- ☐ Break the big problem down into smaller problems.
- ☐ Discuss these problems and possible solutions with your group.
- ☐ What is the best source of information to find out more?

Problem	Solution	How I will find out more
Problem	Solution	How I will find out more
Problem	Solution	How I will find out more

52

Citing references

> Researchers cite (record) their sources of information. This helps to avoid plagiarism (using someone's work without saying it was their idea).

☐ Reflect on all of the information you used to investigate your inquiry.
☐ Cite your sources below.

Type of source (book, website, video, interview …)	Where the source is from (book or website name, title of video …)	Who created it

 What do you notice about your completed table?
Is your research balanced? How might this impact your inquiry?

Ethical use of media literacy

Using media **ethically** creates a safe and happy environment for everyone to enjoy.

Be responsible and kind when using media. Follow the rules and respect other users.

Be honest and check with an adult if you're not sure about something you see or hear.

Be balanced and don't use technology too much. Turn off your devices and do other things.

- Analyse web pages A and B.
- What do you notice?
- How can you identify a reliable website?
- Which might not be safe to use: A or B?

ethically doing something in a way that's correct and fair

54

The Big Basketball Bash

Hundreds of kids from schools in the south of the country are heading to a great event this summer. The Big Basketball Bash is all about raising money for different charities while kids have fun and keep fit.

Interested?
Children can ask their schools to get involved. Teachers can sign their schools up by filling in the form on our website.

Health & safety

Who runs the Big Basketball Bash?

What did you think while you read each web page? Record your thoughts.

 What could be useful to remember next time you look at a web page?

Using media ethically

How reliable is your information?

☐ Reflect on the sources you used for your research.
☐ Identify which sources seemed most/least reliable. Order them in the boxes.
☐ Explain why you feel this way.

Most reliable ↑

Source of information:

Source of information:

Source of information:

↓ Least reliable

What makes you say that?

💬 Discuss your thoughts with your group.
Think of some key rules to follow when researching.

Taking action

I am planning an inquiry into:

....

....

....

What are we learning about? (concepts, subjects)			
Which skills are our tools for this learning?			
These skills help us to be … (learner profile attributes)			
What action can we take to show our understanding?			

Exchanging information

An audience can be one person or a room full of people. We use many communication skills to make sure they understand and enjoy what we are saying.

Speak clearly and use simple words to help the audience understand.

Make eye contact to show that you are interested in your audience and make them feel involved.

Move your hands and use your face to help express your feelings and ideas.

How comfortable are you speaking to an audience?
Draw an arrow on the line to show how you feel.

I feel mostly uncomfortable   I am becoming more of a risk-taker   I feel confident and I'm ready to go further

What will help you to improve this communication skill?

58

Following instructions

Instructions:
- ☐ Divide your class into two groups.
- ☐ Group 1 choose an object in the room (such as a desk or a book) and ask Group 2 to provide a definition.
- ☐ Group 1 use critical thinking and look for problems with the definition.
- ☐ Group 2 change the definition to deal with comments made by Group 1.
- ☐ Group 1 continue to feed back and Group 2 continue to make changes until everyone is happy with the definition.

Reflect on your speaking and listening skills as you completed the task above. Which part of this activity did you find most difficult?

- Listening?
- Reading?
- Following instructions?
- Responding to others?
- Speaking in a group?

Share your reflection here.

Understanding feedback

When someone gives you feedback or constructive criticism, they are giving you advice on how to improve, which can help you learn and grow. It helps you see things from different perspectives and makes you more **open-minded**.

What does constructive criticism mean to you?

How do you feel about constructive criticism?

☐ I don't like it yet.   ☐ Sometimes I like it. Sometimes I don't.   ☐ I think it is very helpful for everyone.

60

Giving and receiving constructive criticism

Think about constructive criticism.

 Clearly explain your goal to someone.

 Listen carefully. Write down their suggestions.

 Thank them, then go and ask more people!
You can compare everyone's feedback afterwards.

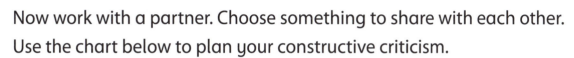

Now work with a partner. Choose something to share with each other.
Use the chart below to plan your constructive criticism.

Before the conversation:	During the conversation:	After the conversation:
• What do you want to say? • What do you want feedback on?	• Take notes. • What makes sense? • What is helpful?	• How will you use the constructive criticism to grow and improve? • What are your action steps?

 How did you feel during this experience? How might this help your learning?

ICT: forms of communication

We use Information and Communication Technology (ICT) to gather, investigate and share information. It is important to choose the right form of technology for different purposes and audiences.

Write which forms of technology you might use in each category.

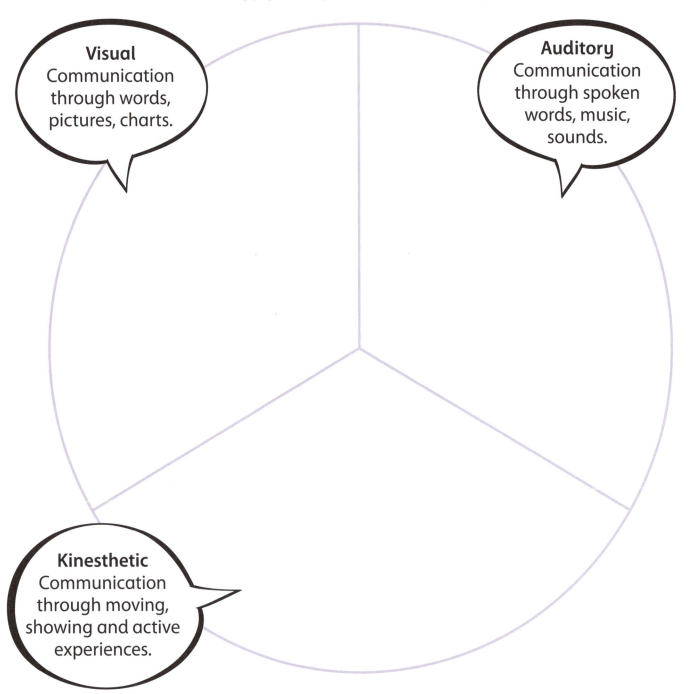

Visual
Communication through words, pictures, charts.

Auditory
Communication through spoken words, music, sounds.

Kinesthetic
Communication through moving, showing and active experiences.

 Reflect on which category or categories you are most comfortable using, and why.

Communicating using ICT

- ☐ Reflect on the different forms of ICT you might use in your next presentation.
- ☐ Think about why you would like to use these forms of ICT.

Which forms of communication are you comfortable using?

Which forms of communication would you like to try?

Literacy: the power of written language

Literacy is being able to read, write, speak and listen to communicate effectively.

In one word, this week was:

....

> List all the things that made the week this way for you.

> Show how you use reading and writing as a way to communicate your thoughts, ideas or problems.

In what areas of literacy would you like to be more of a **risk-taker**?
How could you do this?

Using literacy to communicate

Create a mind map to show all of the ways you could use literacy to communicate your thoughts and ideas within your inquiries and research.

Communicating using technology

Reflect on your inquiry.

Key presentation points:
- Who am I presenting to?
- How can I get their attention?
- What do I want them to know/do/have?
- What is the best way to present my information?

Taking action

Use the chart below to plan how you might take action.

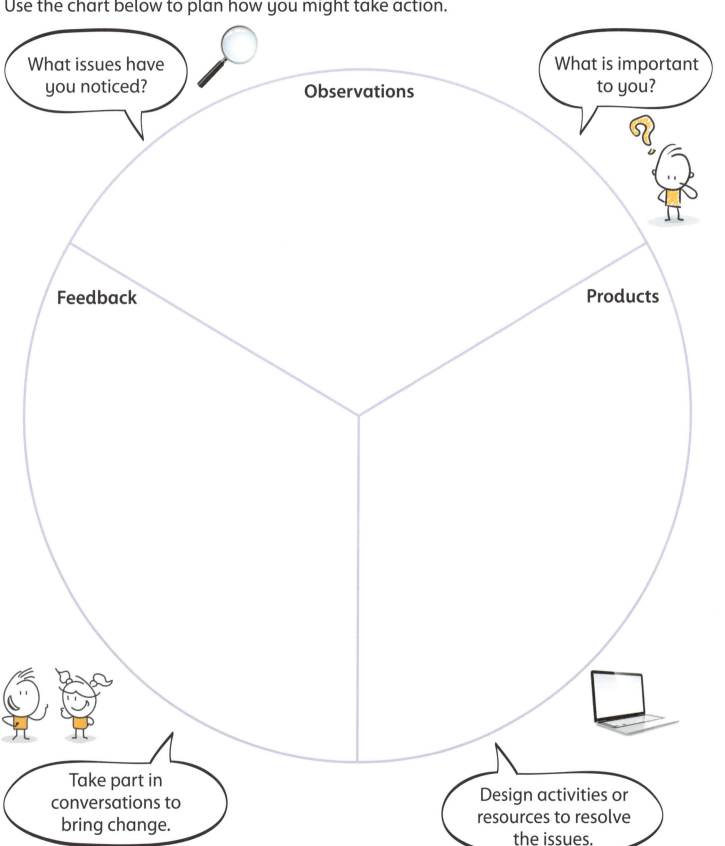

Taking action using the SDGs

The United Nations is a community effort – a global community putting their skills together and collaborating to take action for the greater good.

Choose a problem that you care about:

....

....

How could you work collaboratively to take action?
Which people or organizations could you work with?

How could you take action?

Think about the action categories below and on page 70.

Personal action
What personal action do I want to take?

Community action
What could I do for my local community?

Global action
How can I connect to the SDGs?

What might action look like?

Add your thoughts below.

participation

advocacy

social justice

Taking action using the SDGs

What might action look like? Add your thoughts below.

How could you connect this with your research?

70

What if you could choose two goals to support your action?

I choose:

How do these goals connect with your action plan?

Expressing ideas and opinions: the SDGs

What actions could you take to work towards the goals you chose on the last page?

What three things do you want to do from now on to help the world achieve the SDGs?

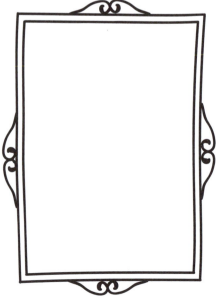

Peace, justice and strong institutions

We need laws and institutions (big organizations) to protect us.

Share your opinion of Goal 16.

What new law would you create for the world if you were in charge?

....

....

....

 Explain your new law to others in your class. How do your new laws compare?

Expressing ideas and opinions: the SDGs

Partnerships for the goals

We must all work together to achieve the SDGs.

Why is this goal important?

How might this goal connect with your learning community?

Reviewing my exhibition

Reflect on your exhibition.

What went well?

What would you do differently?

What did you learn?

Reviewing my exhibition

Reflect on your exhibition.

What scared you?

What did you enjoy?

Reflecting on my year

Something I learned …

Something I am proud of …

The SDG I thought about the most was …

The learner profile attribute that I used the most was …

Reflecting on my year

The book I loved the most was about …

....
....
....
....

A memory I'll keep …

....
....
....
....

This is a drawing of …

....
....
....
....
....

What's next?

Next year, I hope to …

Calming the mind with our breath

Today, we're going to learn a special mindfulness practice to help calm our minds when we are feeling big emotions. Start by finding a comfortable and quiet spot to sit or lie down. Close your eyes if you like, or just look down. Take a moment to become calm.

Take a slow, deep breath in through your nose. Feel your stomach rise. Hold for a moment and then be gentle as you breathe out through your mouth or nose. With each breath out, let go of any part of you that feels tight.

Picture a calm and relaxing colour in your mind. It could be light blue like the sky, or maybe a soft pink like a flower. Imagine this colour all around you, making you feel safe and peaceful.

As you breathe in, imagine you're drawing in this calming colour through your nose. See the colour filling your whole body, reaching all the way to your brain.

Now, as you breathe out, imagine any worries, fears or other big emotions leaving your body as a different colour – maybe grey or black. With each breath out, release these colours and let them slowly disappear.

Keep breathing in the calming colour and breathing out the worries. Imagine you are becoming calmer and happier with each breath.

When you're ready, slowly open your eyes and notice how your body and mind feel. You've just given them some love and care. Remember, whenever you feel a big emotion like fear, worry, anger or sadness, you can use your breath and calming colour to help relax your mind and feel calm and safe.